The Outdoor Life of Children

Charlotte Mason

ISBN: 1508581681
ISBN-13: 978-1508581680

DEDICATION

To parents and teachers everywhere who take time outdoors with children in order to enjoy nature and to learn firsthand about our wonderful world.

CONTENTS

FOREWORD

Nature Study has always been my personal favorite Charlotte Mason topic, and is the backbone of introductory Natural Sciences in Charlotte Mason-inspired homes and classrooms. But Mason also felt it was beneficial for children to spend a great deal of time out-of-doors for their physical, emotional, and spiritual health.

In spite of often rainy, inclement weather, Charlotte Mason insisted on going out once-a-week for an official Nature Walk, allowing the children to experience and observe the natural environment firsthand. These excursions were nature *walks*, not nature *talks*. In addition to these Nature Walks, Mason also recommended children spend large quantities of time outside each day, no matter what the weather. So take a daily walk for fun and fresh air.

From the time children were old enough to keep one, Mason had her students keep a personal Nature Notebook. Nature Notebooks are essentially artist sketchbooks containing pictures the children have personally drawn/painted of plants, wildlife, or other natural objects found in a natural setting. These journals can also include nature-related poetry, prose, detailed descriptions, weather notes, Latin names, etc. I can't stress enough how valuable I've found the Nature Notebook idea. We always tried to remember to take our Nature Notebooks (I kept one, too) with us whenever we'd go on any sort of outdoor adventure.

Our family was never blessed with acres of property off in the country for our children to frolic to their hearts' content, but a small city lot and many local parks offered us tremendous opportunities for outdoor learning activities. To make up for the lack of open natural space in our neighborhood, we went to various local parks at least two to three times per week. We didn't go to the parks for the play equipment, but for the exposure to a more natural setting.

I want to encourage those of you who don't have your own fields and forests, there are other readily available opportunities for outdoor play and learning activities. Basically, go outside with your kids as often as you can. You'll all be healthier, happier, and will learn a thing or two in the process.

Deborah Taylor-Hough
Seattle, 2015

1

A GROWING TIME

Meals Out of Doors

People who live in the country know the value of fresh air very well, and their children live out of doors, with intervals within for sleeping and eating. As to the latter, even country people do not make full use of their opportunities. On fine days when it is warm enough to sit out with wraps, why should not tea and breakfast, everything but a hot dinner, be served out of doors? For we are an overwrought generation, running to nerves as a cabbage runs to seed; and every hour spent in the open is a clear gain, tending to the increase of brain power and bodily vigour, and to the lengthening of life itself. They who know what it is to have fevered skin and throbbing brain deliciously soothed by the cool touch of the air are inclined to make a new rule of life, Never be within doors when you can *rightly* be without.

Besides, the gain of an hour or two in the open air, there is this to be considered: meals taken *al fresco* are usually joyous, and there is nothing like gladness for converting meat and drink into healthy blood and tissue. All the time, too, the children are storing up memories of a happy childhood. Fifty years hence they will see the shadows of the boughs making patterns on the white tablecloth; and sunshine, children's laughter, hum of bees, and scent of flowers are being bottled up for after refreshment.

For Dwellers in Towns and Suburbs

But it is only the people who live, so to speak, in their own gardens who can make a practice of giving their children tea out of doors. For the rest of us, and the most of us, who live in towns or the suburbs of towns, that is included in the larger question—How much time daily in the open air should the children have? And how is it possible to secure this for them? In this time of extraordinary pressure, educational and social, perhaps a mother's first duty to her children is to secure for them a quiet growing time, a full six years of passive receptive life, the waking part of it spent for the most part out in the fresh air. And this, not for the gain in bodily health alone—body and soul, heart and mind, are nourished with food convenient for them when the children are let alone, let to live without friction and without stimulus amongst happy influences which incline them to be good.

Possibilities of a Day in the Open

I make a point, says a judicious mother, of sending my children out, weather permitting, for an hour in the winter, and two hours a day in the summer months. That is well; but it is not enough. In the first place, do not send them; if it is anyway possible, take them; for, although the children should be left much to themselves, there is a great deal to be done and a great deal to be prevented during these long hours in the open air. And long hours they should be; not two, but four, five, or six hours they should have on every tolerably fine day, from April till October. Impossible! Says an overwrought mother who sees her way to no more for her children than a daily hour or so on the pavements of the neighbouring London squares.

Let me repeat, that I venture to suggest, not what is practicable in any household, but what seems to me *absolutely best for the children*; and that, in the faith that mothers work wonders once they are convinced that wonders are demanded of them. A journey of twenty minutes by rail or omnibus, and a luncheon basket, will make a day in the country possible to most town dwellers; and if one day, why not many, even every suitable day?

Supposing we have got them, what is to be done with these golden hours, so that every one shall be delightful? They must be spent with some method, or the mother will be taxed and the children bored. There is a great deal to be accomplished in this large fraction of the children's day. They must be kept in a joyous temper all the time, or they will miss some of the strengthening and refreshing held in charge for them by the blessed air. They must be let alone, left to themselves a great deal, to take in what they can of the beauty of earth and heavens; for of the evils of modern education few are worse than this—that the perpetual cackle of his elders leaves the poor child not a moment of time, nor an inch of space, wherein to wonder—and grow. At the same time, here is the mother's opportunity to train the seeing-eye, the hearing ear, and to drop seeds of truth into the open soul of the child, which shall germinate, blossom, and bear fruit, without further help or knowledge of hers. Then, there is much to be got by perching in a tree or nestling in heather, but muscular development comes of more active ways, and an hour or two should be spent in vigorous play; and last, and truly least, a lesson or two must be got in.

No Story-Books

Let us suppose mother and children arrived at some breezy open wherein it seemeth always afternoon. In the first place, it is not her business to entertain the little people: there should be no story-books, no telling of tales, as little talk as possible, and that to some purpose. Who thinks to amuse children with tale or talk at a circus or pantomime? And here, is there not infinitely more displayed for their delectation? Our wise mother, arrived, first sends the children to let off their spirits in a wild scamper, with cry, hallo, and hullaballo, and any extravagance that comes into their young heads. There is no distinction between big and little; the latter love to follow in the wake of their elders, and, in lessons or play, to pick up and do according to their little might. As for the baby, he is in bliss: divested of his garments, he kicks and crawls, and clutches the grass, laughs soft baby laughter, and takes in his little knowledge of shapes and properties in his own wonderful fashion—clothed in a woolen gown, long and loose, which is none the worse for the worst usage it may get.

Sight-Seeing

By-and-by the others come back to their mother, and, while wits are fresh and eyes are keen, she sends them off on an exploring expedition—Who can see the most, and tell the most, about yonder hillock or brook, hedge, or copse. This is an exercise that delights children, and may be endlessly varied, carried on in the spirit of a game, and yet with the exactness and carefulness of a lesson.

How to See

Find out all you can about that cottage at the foot of the hill; but do not pry about too much. Soon they are back, and there is a crowd of excited faces, and a hubbub of tongues, and random observations are shot breathlessly into the mother's ear. 'There are bee-hives.' 'We saw a lot of bees going into one.' 'There is a long garden.' 'Yes, and there are sunflowers in it.' 'And hen-and-chicken daisies and pansies.' 'And there's a great deal of pretty blue flowers with rough leaves, mother; what do you suppose it is?' 'Borage for the bees, most likely; they are very fond of it.' 'Oh, and there are apple and pear and plum trees on one side; there's a little path up the middle, you know.' 'On which hand side are the fruit trees?' 'The right—no, the left; let me see, which is my thimble-hand? Yes, it is the right-hand side.' 'And there are potatoes and cabbages, and mint and things on the other side.' 'Where are the flowers, then?' 'Oh, they are just the borders, running down each side of the path.' 'But we have not told mother about the wonderful apple tree; I should think there are a million apples on it, all ripe and rosy!' 'A *million*, Fanny?' 'Well, a great many, mother; I don't know how many.' And so on, indefinitely; the mother getting by degrees a complete description of the cottage and its garden.

Educational Uses of Sight-Seeing

This is all play to the children, but the mother is doing invaluable work; she is training their powers of observation and expression, increasing their vocabulary and their range of ideas by giving them the name and the uses of an object at the right moment,—when they ask, 'What is it?' and 'What is it for?' And she is training her children in truthful habits, by making them careful to see the fact and to state it exactly, without omission or exaggeration. The child who describes, 'A tall tree, going up into a point, with rather roundish leaves; not a pleasant tree for shade, because the branches all go up,' deserves to learn the name of the tree, and anything her mother has to tell her about it. But the little bungler, who fails to make it clear whether he is describing an elm or a beech, should get no encouragement; not a foot should his mother move to see his tree, no coaxing should draw her into talk about it, until, in despair, he goes off, and comes back with some more certain note—rough or smooth bark, rough or smooth leaves,—then the mother considers, pronounces, and, full of glee, he carries her off to see for himself.

Discriminating Observation

By degrees the children will learn *discriminatingly* every feature of the landscapes with which they are familiar; and think what a delightful possession for old age and middle life is a series of pictures imaged, feature by feature, in the sunny glow of the child's mind! The miserable thing about the childish recollections of most persons is that they are blurred, distorted, incomplete, no more pleasant to look upon than a fractured cup or a torn garment; and the reason is, not that the old scenes are forgotten, but that they were never fully *seen*. At the time, there was no more than a hazy impression that such and such objects were present, and naturally, after a lapse of years those features can rarely be recalled of which the child was not *cognisant* when he saw them before him.

'Picture-Painting'

So exceedingly delightful is this faculty of taking mental photographs, exact images, of the beauties of Nature we go about the world for the refreshment of seeing, that it is worthwhile to exercise children in another way towards this end, bearing in mind, however, that they see the near and the minute, but can only be made with an effort to look at the wide and the distant. Get the children to look well at some patch of landscape, and then to shut their eyes and call up the picture before them, if any bit of it is blurred, they had better look again. When they have a perfect image before their eyes, let them say what they see. Thus: 'I see a pond; it is shallow on this side, but deep on the other; trees come to the water's edge on that side, and you can see their green leaves and branches so plainly in the water that you would think there was a wood underneath. Almost touching the trees in the water is a bit of blue sky with a soft white cloud; and when you look up you see that same little cloud, but with a great deal of sky instead of a patch, because there are no trees up there. There are lovely little water-lilies round the far edge of the pond, and two or three of the big round leaves are turned up like sails. Near where I am standing three cows have come to drink, and one has got far into the water, nearly up to her neck,' etc.

Strain on the Attention

This, too, is an exercise children delight in, but, as it involves some strain on the attention, it is fatiguing, and should only be employed now and then. It is, however, well worthwhile to give children the habit of getting a bit of landscape by heart in this way, because it is the effort of recalling and reproducing that is fatiguing; while the altogether pleasurable act of seeing, *fully and in detail*, is likely to be repeated unconsciously until it becomes a habit by the child who is required now and then to reproduce what he sees.

Seeing Fully and in Detail

At first the children will want a little help in the art of seeing. The mother will say, 'Look at the reflection of the trees! There might be a wood under the water. What do those standing up leaves remind you of?' And so on, until the children have noticed the salient points of the scene. She will even herself learn off two or three scenes, and describe them with closed eyes for the children's amusement; and such little mimics are they, and at the same time so sympathetic, that any graceful fanciful touch which she throws into her descriptions will be reproduced with variations in theirs.

The children will delight in this game of picture-painting all the more if the mother introduce it by describing some great picture gallery she has seen—pictures of mountains, of moors, of stormy seas, of ploughed fields, of little children at play, of an old woman knitting,—and goes on to say, that though she does not paint her pictures on canvas and have them put in frames, she carries about with her just such a picture gallery; for whenever she sees anything lovely or interesting, she looks at it until she has the picture in her mind's eye; and then she carries it away with her, her own forever, a picture on view just when she wants it.

A Means of After-Solace and Refreshment

It would be difficult to overrate this habit of seeing and storing as a means of after-solace and refreshment. The busiest of us have holidays when we slip our necks out of the yoke and come face to face with Nature, to be healed and blessed by

> *"The breathing balm,*
> *The silence and the calm*
> *Of mute, insensate things."*

This immediate refreshment is open to everybody according to his measure; but it is a mistake to suppose that everybody is able to carry away a refreshing image of that which gives him delight. Only a few can say with Wordsworth, of scenes they have visited

> *"Though absent long,*
> *These forms of beauty have not been to me*
> *As is a landscape to a blind man's eye;*
> *But oft, in lonely rooms, and mid the din*
> *Of towns and cities, I have owed to them,*
> *In hours of weariness, sensations sweet,*
> *Felt in the blood, and felt along the heart;*
> *And passing even into my purer mind,*
> *With tranquil restoration.*

And yet this is no high poetic gift which the rest of us must be content to admire, but a common reward for taking pains in the act of seeing which parents may do a great deal to confer upon their children.

The mother must beware how she spoils the simplicity, the *objective* character of the child's enjoyment, by treating his little descriptions as feats of cleverness to be repeated to his father or to visitors; she had better make a vow to suppress herself, 'to say nothing to nobody,' in his presence at any rate, though the child should show himself a born poet.

2

THE CHILD GETS KNOWLEDGE BY MEANS OF HIS SENSES

Nature's Teaching

Watch a child standing at gaze at some sight new to him—a plough at work, for instance—and you will see he is as naturally occupied as is a babe at the breast; he is, in fact, taking in the *intellectual* food which the working faculty of his brain at this period requires. In his early years the child is all eyes; he observes, or, more truly, he perceives, calling sight, touch, taste, smell, and hearing to his aid, that he may learn all that is discoverable by him about every new thing that comes under his notice.

Everybody knows how a baby fumbles over with soft little fingers, and carries to his mouth, and bangs that it may produce what sound there is in it, the spoon or doll which supercilious grown-up people give him to 'keep him quiet.' The child is at his lessons, and is learning all about it at a rate utterly surprising to the physiologist, who considers how much is implied in the act of 'seeing,' for instance: that to the infant, as to the blind adult restored to sight, there is at first no difference between a flat picture and a solid body,—that the ideas of form and solidity are not obtained by sight at all, but are the judgments of experience.

9

Then, think of the vague passes in the air the little fist makes before it lays hold of the object of desire, and you see how he learns the whereabouts of things, having as yet no idea of direction. And why does he cry for the moon? Why does he crave equally, a horse or a house-fly as an appropriate plaything? Because far and near, large and small, are ideas he has yet to grasp. The child has truly a great deal to do before he is in a condition to 'believe his own eyes'; but Nature teaches so gently, so gradually, so persistently, that he is never overdone, but goes on gathering little stores of knowledge about whatever comes before him.

And this is the process the child should continue for the first few years of his life. Now is the storing time which should be spent in laying up images of things familiar. By-and-by he will have to conceive of things he has never seen: how can he do it except by comparison with things he has seen and knows? By-and-by he will be called upon to reflect, understand, reason; what material will he have, unless he has a magazine of facts to go upon? The child who has been made to observe how high in the heavens the sun is at noon on a summer's day, how low at noon on a day in mid-winter, is able to *conceive* of the great heat of the tropics under a vertical sun, and to *understand* the climate of a place depends greatly upon the mean height the sun reaches above the horizon.

Overpressure

A great deal has been said lately about the danger of overpressure, of requiring too much mental work from a child of tender years. The danger exists; but lies, not in giving the child too much, but in giving him the wrong thing to do, the sort of work for which the present state of his mental development does not fit him. Who expects a boy in petticoats to lift half a hundredweight? But give the child work that Nature intended for him, and the quantity he can get through with ease is practically unlimited. Whoever saw a child tired of seeing, of examining in his own way, unfamiliar things? This is the sort of mental nourishment for which he has an unbounded appetite, because it is that food of the mind on which, for the present, he is meant to grow.

Object Lessons

Now, how far is this craving for natural sustenance met? In infant and kindergarten schools, by the object lesson, which is good so far as it goes, but is sometimes like that bean a day on which the Frenchman fed his horse. The child at home has more new things brought under his noticed, if with less method. Neither at home nor at school is much effort made to set before the child the abundant 'feast of eyes' which his needs demand.

A Child Learns from 'Things'

We older people, partly because of our maturer intellect, partly because of our defective education, get most of our knowledge through the medium of words. We set the child to learn in the same way, and find him dull and slow. Why? Because it is only with a few words in common use that he associates a definite meaning; all the rest are no more to him than the vocables of a foreign tongue. But set him face to face with a *thing*, and he is twenty times as quick as you are in knowledge about it; knowledge of things flies to the mind of a child as steel filings to magnet. And, *pari passu* with his knowledge of things, his vocabulary grows; for it is a law of the mind that what we know, we struggle to express.

This fact accounts for many of the apparently aimless questions of children; they are in quest, not of knowledge, but of *words* to express the knowledge they have. Now, consider what a culpable waste of intellectual energy it is to shut up a child, blessed with this inordinate capacity for seeing and knowing, within the four walls of a house, or the dreary streets of a town. Or suppose that he is let run loose in the country where there is plenty to see, it is nearly as bad to let this great faculty of the child's dissipate itself in random observations for want of method and direction.

The Sense of Beauty Comes from Early Contact with Nature

There is no end to the store of common information, got in such a way that it will never be forgotten, with which an intelligent child may furnish himself before he begins his school career. The boy who can tell you off-hand where to find each of the half-dozen most graceful birches, the three or four finest ash trees in the neighbourhood of his home, has chances in a life a dozen to one compared with the lower, slower intelligence that does not know an elm from an oak—not merely chances of success, but chances of a larger, happier life, for it is curious how certain *feelings* are linked with the mere observation of Nature and natural objects.

"The *aesthetic* sense of the beautiful," says Dr. Carpenter, "of the sublime, of the harmonious, seems in its most elementary form to connect itself immediately with the Perceptions which arise of out of the contact of our minds with external Nature"; while he quotes Dr. Morrell, who says still more forcibly that "All those who have shown a remarkable appreciation of form and beauty date their first impressions from a period lying far behind the existence of definite ideas or verbal instruction."

Most Grown Men Lose the Habit of Observation

Thus, we owe something to Mr. Evans for taking his little daughter Mary Anne with him on his long business drives among the pleasant Warwickshire lanes; the little girl stood up between her father's knees, seeing much and saying little; and the outcome was the scenes of rural life in *Adam Bede* and *The Mill on the Floss*. Wordsworth, reared amongst the mountains, becomes a very prophet of Nature; while Tennyson draws endless imagery from the levels of the eastern counties where he was brought up. Little David Copperfield was "a very observant child, though," says he, "I think the memory of most of us can go farther back into such times than many of us suppose; just as I believe the power of observation in numbers of very young children to be quite wonderful for its closeness and accuracy. Indeed, I think that most grown men who are remarkable in this respect may with greater propriety be said not to have lost the faculty, than to have acquired it; the rather, as I generally observe such men to retain a certain freshness, and gentleness, and capacity of being pleased, which are also an inheritance they have preserved from their childhood";—in which remark Dickens makes his hero talk sound philosophy as well as kindly sense.

The Child Should Be Made Familiar with Natural Objects

But what is the use of being a 'very observant child,' if you are not put in the way of things worth observing? And here is the difference between the streets of a town and the sights and sounds of the country. There is plenty to be seen in a town and children accustomed to the ways of the streets become nimble-witted enough. But the scraps of information to be picked up in a town are isolated fragments; they do not hang on to anything else, nor come to anything more; the information may be convenient, but no one is the wiser for knowing which side of the street is Smith's, and which turning leads to Thompson's shop.

Every Natural Object a Member of a Series

Now take up a natural object, it does not matter what, and you are studying one of a group, a member of a series; whatever knowledge you get about it is so much towards the *science* which includes all of its kind. Break off an elder twig in the spring; you notice a ring of wood round a centre of pith, and there you have at a glance a distinguishing character of a great division of the vegetable world. You pick up a pebble. Its edges are perfectly smooth and rounded: why? You ask. It is water-worn, weatherworn. And that little pebble brings you face to face with *disintegration*, the force to which, more than to any other, we owe the aspects of the world which we call *picturesque*—glen, ravine, valley, hill. It is not necessary that the child should be told anything about disintegration or dicotyledon, only that he should *observe* the wood and pith in the hazel twig, the pleasant roundness of the pebble; by-and-by he will learn the bearing of the facts with which he is already familiar—a very different thing from learning the reason why of facts which have never come under his notice.

Power Will Pass, More and More, into the Hands of Scientific Men

It is infinitely well worth the mother's while to take some pains every day to secure, in the first place, that her children spend hours daily amongst rural and natural objects; and, in the second place, to infuse into them, or rather to cherish in them, the love of investigation. "I say it deliberately," says Kingsley, "as a student of society and of history: power will pass more and more into the hands of scientific men. They will rule, and they will act—

cautiously, we may hope, and modestly, and charitably—because in learning true knowledge they will have learnt also their own ignorance, and the vastness, the complexity, the mystery of Nature. But they will also be able to rule, they will be able to act, because they have taken the trouble to learn the facts and the laws of Nature."

Intimacy with Nature Makes for Personal Well-being

But to enable them to swim with the stream is the least of the benefits this early training should confer on the children; a love of Nature, implanted so early that it will seem to them hereafter to have been born in them, will enrich their lives with pure interests, absorbing pursuits, health, and good humour. "I have seen," says the same writer, "the young man of fierce passions and uncontrollable daring expend healthily that energy which threatened daily to plunge him into recklessness, if not into sin, upon hunting out and collecting, through rock and bog, snow and tempest, every bird and egg of the neighbouring forest . . . I have seen the young London beauty, amid all the excitement and temptation of luxury and flattery, with her heart pure, and her mind occupied in a boudoir full of shells and fossils, flowers and seaweeds, keeping herself unspotted from the world, by considering the lilies of the fields of the field, how they grow."

3

THE CHILD AND THE MOTHER-NATURE

The Mother Must Refrain from too Much Talk

Does so wide a programme alarm the mother? Does she with dismay see herself talking through the whole of those five or six hours, and, even at that, not getting through a tithe of the teaching laid out for her? On the contrary, the less she says the better; and as for the quantity of educational work to be got through, it is the fable of the anxious pendulum over again: it is true there are countless 'ticks' to be ticked, but there will be always be a second of time to tick in, and no more than a single tick is to be delivered in any given second.

Making a New Acquaintance

The rapid little people will have played their play, whether of 'sight-seeing' or 'picture-painting,' in a quarter of an hour or so; for the study of natural objects, an occasional 'Look!' an attentive examination of the object on the mother's own part, a name given, a remark—a dozen words long—made at the right moment, and the children have begun a new acquaintance which they will prosecute for themselves; and not more than one or two such presentations should occur in a single day.

Now, see how much leisure there is left! The mother's real difficulty will be to keep herself from much talk with the children, and to hinder them from occupying themselves with her. There are few things sweeter and more precious to the child than playful prattle with her mother; but one thing is better—the communing with the larger Mother, in order to which the child and she should be left to themselves. This is, truly, a delightful thing to watch: the mother reads her book or knits her sock, checking all attempts to make talk; the child stares up into a tree, or down into a flower— doing nothing, thinking of nothing; or leads a bird's life among the branches, or capers about in aimless ecstasy;—quite foolish, irrational doings, but, all the time a *fashioning* is going on: Nature is doing *her* part, with the vow—

> *"This child I to myself will take:*
> *She shall be mine, and I will make*
> *A lady of my own."*

Two Things Permissible to the Mother

There is one thing the mother will allow herself to do as interpreter between Nature and the child, but that not oftener than once a week or once a month, and with look and gesture of delight rather than with flow of improving words—she will point out to the child some touch of especial loveliness in colouring or grouping in the landscape or the heavens. One other thing she will do, but very rarely, and with tender filial reverence (most likely she will say her prayers, and speak out of her prayer, for to touch on this ground with *hard* words is to wound the soul of the child): she will point to some lovely flower or gracious tree, not only as a beautiful, but a beautiful *thought* of God, in which we may believe He finds continual pleasure, and which He is pleased to see his human children rejoice in. Such a seed of sympathy with the Divine thought sown in the heart of the child is worth many of the sermons the man may listen to hereafter, much of the 'divinity' he may read.

Out-Of-Door Games, etc.

The bright hours fly by; and there is still at least one lesson on the programme, to say nothing of an hour or two for games in the afternoon. The thought of a *lesson* is uninviting after the discussion of much that is more interesting, and, truly, more important; but it need only be a little lesson, ten minutes long, and the slight break and the effort of attention will give the greater zest to the pleasure and leisure to follow.

The French Lesson

The daily French lesson is that which should not be omitted. That children should learn French *orally*, by listening to and repeating French words and phrases; that they should begin so young that the difference of accent does not strike them, but they repeat the new French word all the same as if it were English and use it as freely; that they should learn a few—two or three, five or six—new French words daily, and that, at the same time, the old words should be kept in use—are points to be considered more fully hereafter: in the meantime, it is so important to keep tongue and ear familiar with French vocables, that not a lesson should be omitted. The French lesson may, however, be made to fit in with the spirit of the other out-of-door occupations; the half-dozen words may be the parts—leaves, branches, bark, trunk of a tree, or the colours of the flowers, or the movements of bird, cloud, lamb, child; in fact, the new French words should be but another form of expression for the ideas that for the time fill the child's mind.

Noisy Games

The afternoon's games, after luncheon, are an important part of the day's doings for the elder children, though the younger have probably worn themselves out by this time with the ceaseless restlessness by means of which Nature provides for the due development of muscular tissue in them; let them sleep in the sweet air, and awake refreshed. Meanwhile, the elders play; the more they run, and shout, and toss their arms, the more healthful is the play. And this is one reason why mothers should carry their children off to lonely places, where they may use their lungs to their hearts' content without risk of annoying anybody. The *muscular* structure of the organs of voice is not enough considered; children love to indulge in cries and shouts and view-halloos, and this 'rude' and 'noisy' play, with which their elders have not much patience, is no more than Nature's way of providing for the due exercise of organs, upon whose working power the health and happiness of the child's future largely depend. People talk of 'weak lungs,' 'weak chest,' 'weak throat,' but perhaps it does not occur to everybody that strong lungs and strong throat are commonly to be had on the same terms as a strong arm or wrist—by exercise, training, *use*, work. Still, if the children can 'give voice' musically, and more rhythmically to the sound of their own voices, so much the better. In this respect French children are better off than English; they dance and sing through a hundred roundelays—just such games, no doubt, mimic marryings and buryings, as the children played at long ago in the market place of Jerusalem.

'Rondes'

Before Puritan innovations made us a staid and circumspect people, English lads and lasses of all ages danced out little dramas on the village green, accompanying themselves with the words and airs of just such *rondes* as the French children sing to-day. We have a few of them left still—to be heard at Sunday school treats and other gatherings of the children,—and they are well worth preserving: 'There came three dukes a-riding, a-riding, a-riding': 'Oranges and lemons, say the bells of St. Clement's'; 'Here we come gathering nuts in May'; 'What has my poor prisoner done?' and many more, all set to delightful sing-song airs that little feet trip to merrily, the more so for the pleasant titillation of the words—dukes, nuts, oranges,—who could not go to the tune of such ideas?

The promoters of the kindergarten system have done much to introduce games of this, or rather of a more educational kind; but is it not a fact that the singing games of the kindergarten are apt to be somewhat inane? Also, it is doubtful how far the prettiest plays, learnt at school and from a teacher, will take hold of the children as do the games which have been passed on from hand to hand through an endless chain of children, and are not be found in the print-books at all.

Skipping-Rope and Shuttlecock

Cricket, tennis, and rounders are *the* games *par excellence* if the children are old enough to play them, both as giving free harmonious play to the muscles, and also as serving the highest moral purpose of games in bringing the children under the discipline of rules; but the little family we have in view, all of them under nine, will hardly be up to scientific games. Races and chases, 'tag,' 'follow my leader,' and any romping game they may invent, will be more to their minds: still better are the hoop, the ball, the shuttlecock, and the invaluable skipping-rope. For the rope, the very best use is to skip with her own, throwing it *backwards* rather than forwards, so that the tendency of the movement is to expand the chest. Shuttlecock is a fine game, affording scope for ambition and emulation. Her biographer thinks it worth telling that Miss Austen could keep up in 'cup and ball' over a hundred times, to the admiration of nephews and nieces; in like manner, any feat in keeping up the shuttle-cock might be noted down as a family event, so that the children may be fired with ambition to excel in a game which affords most graceful and vigorous play to almost every muscle of the upper part of the body, and has this great recommendation, that it can be as well played within doors as without. Quite the best play is to keep up the shuttlecock with a battledore in each hand, so that the muscles on either side are brought equally into play. But to 'ordain' about children's games is an idle waste of words, for here fashion is as supreme and as arbitrary as in questions of bonnet or crinoline.

Climbing

Climbing is an amusement not much in favour with mothers; torn garments, bleeding knees, and boot-toes rubbed into holes, to say nothing of more serious risks, make a strong case against this form of delight. But, truly, the exercise is so admirable––the body being thrown into endless graceful postures which bring every muscle into play,—and the training in pluck, daring, and resource so invaluable that it is a pity trees and cliffs and walls should be forbidden even to little girls.

The mother may do a good deal to avert serious mishaps by accustoming the younger children to small feats of leaping and climbing, so that they learn, at the same time, courage and caution from their own experiences, and are less likely to follow the lead of too-daring playmates. Later, the mother had best make up her mind to share the feelings of the hen that hatched a brood of ducklings, remembering that a little scream and sudden 'Come down instantly!' 'Tommy, you'll break your neck!' gives the child a nervous shock, and is likely to cause the fall it was meant to hinder by startling Tommy out of all presence of mind.

Even boating and swimming are not without the reach of town-bred children, in days when everybody goes for a summer outing to the neighbourhood of the sea or of inland waters; and then, there are swimming baths in most towns. It would be well if most children of seven were taught to swim, not only for the possible usefulness of the art, but as giving them an added means of motion, and, therefore, of delight.

Clothing

The havoc of clothes need not be great if the children are dressed for their little excursions, as they should be, in plainly made garments of some loosely woven woolen material, serge or flannel. Woolen has many advantages over cotton, and more over linen, as a clothing material; chiefly, that it is a bad conductor; that is to say, it does not allow the heat of the body too free an exit, nor the heat of the sun too free an entrance. Therefore the child in woolen, who has become heated in play, does not suffer a chill from the sudden loss of this heat, as does the child in linen garments; also, he is cooler in the sunshine, and warmer in the shade.

4

OUT-OF-DOOR GEOGRAPHY

Small Things May Teach Great

After this long digression, intended to impress upon mothers the supreme importance of stirring up in their children a love of Nature and of natural objects—a deep-seated spring to send up pure waters into the driest places of after-life—we must return to the mother whom we have left out of doors all this time, waiting to know what she is to do next. This pleasant earth of ours is not to be overlooked in the out-of-door education of the children. 'How do you get time for so much?' 'Oh, I leave out subjects of no educational value; I do not teach geography, for instance,' said an advanced young theorist with all sorts of certificates.

Pictorial Geography

But the mother, who knows better, will find a hundred opportunities to teach geography by the way: a duck-pond is a lake or an inland sea; any brooklet will serve to illustrate the great rivers of the world; a hillock grows into a mountain—an Alpine system; a hazel-copse suggests the mighty forests of the Amazon; a reedy swamp, the rice-fields of China; a meadow, the boundless prairies of the West; the pretty purple flowers of the common mallow is a text whereon to hang the cotton fields of the Southern States: indeed, the whole field of pictorial geography—maps may wait until by-and-by—may be covered in this way.

The Position of the Sun

And not only this: the children should be taught to observe the position of the sun in the heavens from hour to hour, and by his position, to tell the time of day. Of course they will want to know why the sun is such an indefatigable traveler, and thereby hangs a wonderful tale, which they may as well learn in the 'age of faith,' of the relative sizes of sun and earth, and of the nature and movements of the latter.

Clouds, Rain, Snow, and Hail

"Clouds and rain, snow and hail, winds and vapours, fulfilling His Word"—are all everyday mysteries that the mother will be called upon to explain faithfully, however simply. There are certain ideas which children must get from within a walking radius of their own home if ever they are to have a real understanding of maps and of geographical terms.

Distance is one of these, and the first idea of distance is to be attained by what children find a delightful operation. A child walks at his usual pace; somebody measures and tells him the length of his pace, and then he measures the paces of his brothers and sisters. Then such a walk, such a distance, here and there, is solemnly paced, and a little sum follows—so many inches or feet covered by each pace equals so many yards in the whole distance. Various short distances about the child's home should be measured in this way; and when the idea of covering distance is fully established, the idea of times as a means of measurement should be introduced. The time taken to pace a hundred yards should be noted down. Having found out that it takes two minutes to pace a hundred yards, children will be able for the next step—that if they have walked for thirty minutes, the walk should measure fifteen hundred yards; in thirty-five minutes they would have walked a mile, or rather seventeen hundred and fifty yards, and then they could add the ten yards more which would make a mile. The longer the legs the longer the pace, and most grown people can walk a mile in twenty minutes.

Direction

By the time they have got somewhat familiar with the idea of distance, that of direction should be introduced. The first step is to make children observant of the progress of the sun. The child who observes the sun for a year and notes down for himself, or dictates, the times of his rising and setting for the greater part of the year, and the points of his rising and setting, will have secured a basis for a good deal of definite knowledge. Such observation should take in the reflection of the sun's light, the evening light reflected by east windows, the morning light by west windows, the varying length and intensity of shadows, the cause of shadows, to be learned by the shadow cast by a figure between the blind and a candle. He should associate, too, the hot hours of the day with the sun high overhead, and the cool hours of the morning and evening with a low sun; and should be reminded, that if he stands straight before the fire, he feels the heat more than if he were in a corner of the room. When he is prepared by a little observation in the course of the sun, he is ready to take in the idea of direction, which depends entirely upon the sun.

East and West

Of course the first two ideas are that the sun rises in the east and sets in the west; from this fact he will be able to tell the direction in which the places near his own home, or the streets of his own town, lie. Bid him stand so that his right is towards the east where the sun rises, and his left towards the west where the sun sets. Then he is looking towards the north and his back is towards the south. All the houses, streets and towns on his right hand are to the east of him, those on the left are to the west. The places he must walk straight forward to reach are north of him, and the places behind him are to the south. If he is in a place new to him where he has never seen the sun rise or set and wants to know in what direction a certain road runs, he must notice in what direction his own shadow falls at twelve o'clock, because at noon the shadows of all objects fall towards the north. Then if he face the north, he has, as before, the south behind him, the east on his right hand, the west on his left; or if he face the sun at noon, he faces south.

Practice in Finding Direction

This will throw an interesting light for him on the names of our great railways. A child may become ready in noticing the directions of places by a little practice. Let him notice how each of the windows of his schoolroom faces, or the windows of each of the rooms in his home; the rows of houses he passes in his walks, and which are north, south, east and west sides of the churches he knows. He will soon be prepared to notice the direction of the wind by noticing the smoke from the chimneys, the movement of branches, corn, grass, etc. If the wind blow from the north—'The north wind doth blow and we shall have snow.' If it blow from the west, a west wind, we expect rain. Care must be taken at this point to make it clear to the child that the wind is named after the quarter it comes from, and not from the point it blows towards—just as he is English because he was born in England, and not French because he goes to France. The ideas of distance and direction may now be combined. Such a building is two hundred yards to the east of a gate, such a village two miles to the west. He will soon come across the difficulty, that a place is not exactly east or west, north or south. It is well to let him give, in a round-about way, the direction of places as—'more to the east than the west, 'very near the east but not quite,' 'half-way between east and west.' He will value the exact means of expression all the more for having felt the need of them.

Later, he should be introduced to the wonders of the mariner's compass, should have a little pocket compass of his own, and should observe the four cardinal and all other points. These will afford him the names for directions that he has found it difficult to describe.

Compass Drill

Then he should do certain compass drills in this way: Bid him hold the N of the compass towards the north. "Then, with the compass in your hand, turn towards the east, and you will see a remarkable thing. The little needle moves, too, but moves quite by itself in just the other direction. Turn to the west, and again the needle moves in the opposite direction to that in which you move. However little you turn, a little quiver of the needle follows your movement. And you look at it, wondering how the little thing could perceive you had moved, when you hardly knew it yourself. Walk straight on in any direction, and the needle is fairly steady; only fairly steady, because you are sure, without intending it, to move a little to the right or left. Turn round very slowly, a little bit at a time, beginning at the north and turning towards the east, and you may make the needle also move round in a circle. It moves in the opposite direction to yourself, for it is trying to get back to the north from which you are turning."

Boundaries

The children having got the idea of direction, it will be quite easy to introduce that of boundaries—such and such a turnip field, for instance, is bounded by the highroad on the south, by a wheat crop on the south-east, a hedge on the north-east, and so on; the children getting by degrees the idea that the boundaries of a given space are simply whatever touches it on every side. Thus one crop may touch another without any dividing line, and therefore one crop bounds the other. It is well that children should get clear notions on this subject, or, later, they will be vague when they learn that such a county is 'bounded' by so and so. In connection with bounded spaces whether they be villages, towns, ponds, fields, or what not, children should be led to notice the various crops raised in the district, why pasture-lands and why cornfields, what manner of rocks appear, and how many sorts of tree grow in the neighbourhood. For every field or other space that is examined, that they should draw a rude plan in the sand, giving the shape roughly and lettering the directions as N, S, W, etc.

Plans

By-and-by, when they have learned to draw plans indoors, they will occasionally pace the length of a field and draw their plan according to scale, allowing an inch for five or for ten yards. The ground-plans of garden, stables, house, etc. might follow.

Local Geography

It is probable that a child's own neighbourhood will give him opportunities to learn the meaning of hill and dale, pool and brook, watershed, the current, bed, banks, tributaries of a brook, the relative positions of villages and towns; and all this local geography he must be able to figure roughly on a plan done with chalk on a rock, or with walking stick in the gravel, perceiving the relative distances and situations of the places he marks.

5

FLOWERS AND TREES

Children Should Know Field-crops

In the course of this 'sight-seeing' and 'picture-painting,' opportunities will occur to make the children familiar with rural objects and employments. If there are farm-lands within reach, they should know meadow and pasture, clover, turnip, and corn field, under every aspect, from the ploughing of the land to the getting in of the crops.

Field Flowers and the Life-History of Plants

Milkwort, eyebright, rest-harrow, lady's-bedstraw, willow-herb, every wild flower that grows in their neighbourhood, they should know quite well; should be able to describe the leaf—its shape, size, growing from the root or from the stem; the manner of flowering—a head of flowers, a single flower, a spike, etc. And, having made the acquaintance of a wild flower, so that they can never forget it or mistake it, they should examine the spot where they find it, so that they will know for the future in what sort of ground to look for such and such a flower. 'We should find wild thyme here!' 'Oh, this is the very spot for marsh marigolds; we must come here in the spring.' If the mother is no great botanist, she will find Miss Ann Pratt's *Wild Flowers* very useful, with its coloured plates, like enough to identify the flowers, by common English names, and pleasant facts and fancies that the children delight in. To make collections of wild flowers for the several months, press them, and mount them neatly on squares of cartridge paper, with the English name, habitat, and date of finding each, affords much happy occupation and, at the same time, much useful training: better still is it to accustom children to make careful brush drawings for the flowers that interest them, of the whole plant where possible.

The Study of Trees

Children should be made early intimate with the trees, too; should pick out half a dozen trees, oak, elm, ash, beech, in their winter nakedness, and take these to be their year-long friends. In the winter, they will observe the light tresses of the birch, the knotted arms of the oak, the sturdy growth of the sycamore. They may wait to learn the names of the trees until the leaves come. By-and-by, as the spring advances, behold a general stiffening and look of life in the still bare branches; life stirs in the beautiful mystery of the leaf-buds, a nest of delicate baby leaves lying in downy warmth within many waterproof wrappings; oak and elm, beech and birch, each has its own way of folding and packing its leaflets; observe the 'ruby budded lime' and the ash, with its pretty stag's foot of a bud, not green but black—

"More black than ash-buds in the front of March."

The Seasons Should be Followed

But it is hard to keep pace with the wonders that unfold themselves in the 'bountiful season bland.' There are the dangling catkins and the little ruby eyed pistil-late flowers of the hazel—clusters of flowers, both of them, two sorts on a single tree; and the downy staminate catkins of the willow; and the festive breaking out of all the trees into lovely leafage; the learning the patterns of the leaves as they come out, and the naming of the trees from this and other signs. Then the flowers come, each shut up tight in the dainty casket we call a bud, as cunningly wrapped as the leaves in their buds, but less carefully guarded, for these 'sweet nurslings' delay their coming for the most part until earth has a warm bed to offer, and the sun a kindly welcome.

Leigh Hunt on Flowers

"Suppose," says Leigh Hunt, "suppose flowers themselves were new! Suppose they had just come into the world, a sweet reward for some new goodness... Imagine what we should feel when we saw the first lateral stem bearing off from the main one, and putting forth a leaf. How we should watch the leaf gradually unfolding its little graceful hand; then another, then another; then the main stalk rising and producing more; then one of them giving indications of the astonishing novelty—a bud! then this mysterious bud gradually unfolding like the leaf, amazing us, enchanting us, almost alarming us with delight, as if we knew not what enchantment were to ensue, till at length, in all its fairy beauty, and odorous voluptuousness, and the mysterious elaboration of tender and living sculpture, shines forth the blushing flower." The *flowers*, it is true, are not new; but the *children* are; and it is the fault of their elders if every new flower they come upon is not to them a *Picciola*, a mystery of beauty to be watched from day to day with unspeakable awe and delight.

Meanwhile, we have lost sight of those half-dozen forest-trees which the children have taken into a sort of comradeship for the year. Presently they have the delight of discovering that the great trees have flowers, too, flowers very often of the same hue as their leaves, and that some trees have put off having their leaves until their flowers have come and gone. By-and-by there is the fruit, and the discovery that every tree—with exceptions which they need not learn yet—and every plant bears fruit, 'fruit and seed after his kind.' All this is stale knowledge to older people, but one of the secrets of the educator is to present nothing as stale knowledge, but to put himself in the position of the child, and wonder and admire with him; for every common miracle which the child sees with his own eyes makes of him for the moment another Newton.

Calendars

It is a capital plan for the children to keep a calendar—the first oak-leaf, the first tadpole, the first cowslip, the first catkin, the first ripe blackberries, where seen, and when. The next year they will know when and where to look out for their favourites, and will, every year, be in a condition to add new observations. Think of the zest and interest, the *object*, which such a practice will give to daily walks and little excursions. There is hardly a day when some friend may not be expected to hold a first 'At Home.'

Nature Diaries

As soon as he is able to keep it himself, a nature-diary is a source of delight to a child. Every day's walk gives him something to enter: three squirrels in a larch tree, a jay flying across such a field, a caterpillar climbing up a nettle, a snail eating a cabbage leaf, a spider dropping suddenly to the ground, where he found ground ivy, how it was growing and what plants were growing with it, how bindweed or ivy manages to climb. Innumerable matters to record occur to the intelligent child.

While he is quite young (five or six), he should begin to illustrate his notes freely with brush drawings; he should have a little help at first in mixing colours, in the way of principles, not directions. He should not be told to use now this and now that, but, 'we get purple by mixing so and so,' and then he should be left to himself to get the right tint. As for drawing, instruction has no doubt its time and place; but his nature diary should be left to his own initiative. A child of six will produce a dandelion, poppy, daisy, iris, with its leaves, impelled by the desire to represent what he sees, with surprising vigour and correctness.

An exercise book with stiff covers serves for a nature diary, but care is necessary in choosing paper that answers both for writing and brush drawing.

'I can't stop thinking.'

'But I can't stop thinking; I can't make my mind to sit down!' Poor little girl! All children owe you thanks for giving voice to their dumb woes. And we grown-up people have so little imagination, that we send a little boy with an over-active brain to play by himself in the garden in order to escape the fag of lessons.

Little we know how the brain-people swarm in and out and rush about!

"The human (brain) is like a millstone, turning ever round and round;
If it have nothing else to grind, it must itself be ground."

Set the child to definite work by all means, and give him something to grind. But, pray, let him work with things and not with signs—the things of Nature in their own places, meadow and hedgerow, woods and shore.

6

'LIVING CREATURES'

A Field of Interest and Delight

Then, as for the 'living creatures,' here is a field of unbounded interest and delight. The domesticated animals are soon taken into kindly fellowship by the little people. Perhaps they live too far from the 'real country' for squirrels and wild rabbits to be more to them than a dream of possible delights. But surely there is a pond within reach—by road or rail—where tadpoles may be caught, and carried home in a bottle, fed, and watched through all their changes—fins disappearing, tails getting shorter and shorter, until at last there is no tail at all, and a pretty pert little frog looks you in the face.

Turn up any chance stone, and you may come upon a colony of ants. We have always known that it becomes us to consider their ways and be wise; but now, think of all Lord Avebury has told us to make that twelve-year-old ant of his acquaintance quite a personage. Then, there are the bees. Some of us may have heard the late Dean Farrar describe that lesson he was present at, on 'How doth the little busy bee'— the teacher bright, but the children not responsive; they took no interest at all in little busy bees. He suspected the reason, and questioning the class, found that not one of them had ever seen a bee. 'Had never seen a bee! Think for a moment,' said he, 'of how much that implies'; and then we were moved by an eloquent picture of the sad child-life from which bees and birds and flowers are all shut out. But how many children are there who do not live in the slums of London, and yet are unable to distinguish a bee from a wasp, or even a 'humble' from a honey-bee!

Children Should be Encouraged to Watch

Children should be encouraged to *watch*, patiently and quietly, until they learn something of the habits and history of bee, ant, wasp, spider, hairy caterpillar, dragon-fly, and whatever of larger growth comes in their way. 'The creatures never have any habits while I am looking!' a little girl in some story-book is made to complain; but that was her fault; the bright keen eyes with which children are blest were made to see, and see into, the doings of creatures too small for the unaided observation of older people.

Ants may be brought under home observation in the following way: Get two pieces of glass 1 foot square, three strips of glass 11½ inches long, and one strip 11 inches long, these all ¼ - inch wide. The glass must be carefully cut so as to fit exactly. Place the four strips of glass upon one of the sheets of glass and fix in an exact square, leaving a ½-inch opening, with seccotine or any good fixer. Get from an ant-hill about twelve ants (the yellow ants are best, as the red are inclined to be quarrelsome), a few eggs, and one queen. The queen will be quite as large as an ordinary ant, and so can be easily seen. Take some of the earth of the ant-hill. Put the earth with your ants and eggs upon the sheet of glass and fix the other sheet above, leaving only the small hole in one corner, made by the shorter strip, which should be stopped with a bit of cotton-wool. The ants will be restless for perhaps forty-eight hours, but will then begin to settle and arrange the earth. Remove the wool plug once a week, and replace it after putting two or three drops of honey on it. Once in three weeks remove the plug to drop in with a syringe about ten drops of water. This will not be necessary in the winter while the ants are asleep. This 'nest' will last for years.

With regard to the horror which some children show of beetle, spider, worm, that is usually a trick picked up from grown-up people. Kingsley's children would run after their 'daddy' with a 'delicious worm,' a 'lovely toad,' a 'sweet beetle' carried tenderly in both hands. There are real antipathies not to be overcome, such as

Kingsley's own horror of a spider; but children who are accustomed to hold and admire caterpillars and beetles from their babyhood will not give way to affected horrors. The child who spends an hour in watching the ways of some new 'grub' he has come upon will be a man of mark yet. Let all he finds out about it be entered in his diary—by his mother, if writing be a labour to him,—where he finds it, what it is doing, or seems to him to be doing; its colour, shape, legs: someday he will come across the name of the creature, and will recognise the description of an old friend.

The Force of Public Opinion in the Home

Some children are born naturalists, with a bent inherited, perhaps, from an unknown ancestor; but every child has a natural interest in the living things about him which it is the business of his parents to encourage; for, but few children are equal to holding their own in the face of public opinion; and if they see that the things which interest them are indifferent or disgusting to you, their pleasure in them vanishes, and that chapter in the book of Nature is closed to them. It is likely that the *Natural History of Selborne* would never have been written had it not been that the naturalist's father used to take his boys on daily foraging expeditions, when not a moving or growing thing, not a pebble nor a boulder within miles of Selborne, escaped their eager examination.

Audubon, the American ornithologist, is another instance of the effect of this kind of early training. "When I had hardly learned to walk," he says, "and to articulate those first words always so endearing to parents, the productions of Nature that lay spread all around were constantly pointed out to me . . . My father generally accompanied my steps, procured birds and flowers for me, and pointed out the elegant movements of the former, the beauty and softness of their plumage, the manifestations of their pleasure, or their sense of danger, and the always perfect forms and splendid attire of the latter. He would speak of the departure and return of the birds with the season, describe their haunts, and, more wonderful than all, their change of livery, thus exciting me to study them, and to raise my mind towards their great Creator."

What Town Children Can Do

Town children may get a great deal of pleasure in watching the ways of sparrows—knowing little birds, and easily tamed by a dole of crumbs,—and their days out will bring them in the way of new acquaintances. But much may be done with sparrows. A friend writes:—"Have you seen the man in the gardens of Tuileries feeding and talking to dozens of them? They sit on his hat, his hands, and feed from his fingers. When he raises his arms they all flutter up and then settle again on him and round him. I have watched him call a sparrow from a distance by name and refuse food to all others till *'petit chou,'* a pretty pied sparrow, came for his destined bit. Others had their names and came at call, but I could not see any distinguishing feature; and the crowd of sparrows on the walk, benches and railing, formed a most attentive audience to the bright French talk which kept them in constant motion as they were, here one and there another, invited to come for a tempting morsel. Truly a St. Francis and the birds!"

The child who does not know the portly form and spotted breast of the thrush, the graceful flight of the swallow, the yellow bill of the blackbird, the gush of song which the skylark pours from above, is nearly as much to be pitied as those London children who 'had never seen a bee.' A pleasant acquaintance, easy to pick up, is the hairy caterpillar. The moment to seize him is when he is seen shuffling along the ground in a great hurry; he is on the look-out for quiet quarters in which to lie up: put him in a box, then, and cover the box with net, through which you may watch his operations. Food does not matter—he has other things to attend to. By-and-by he spins a sort of white tent or hammock, into which he retires; you may see through it and watch him, perhaps at the very moment when his skin splits asunder, leaving him, for months to come, an egg-shaped mass without any sign of life. At last the living thing within breaks out of this bundle, and there it is, the handsome tiger-moth, fluttering feeble wings against the net. Most children of six have had this taste of a naturalist's experience, and it is worth speaking of only because, instead of being merely a harmless amusement, it is a valuable piece of education, of more use to the child than the reading of a whole book of natural history, or much geography and Latin. For the evil is, that children get their knowledge of natural history, like all their knowledge, at second hand. They are so sated with wonders, that nothing surprises them; and they are so little used to see for themselves, that nothing interests them. The cure for this *blasé* condition is, to let them alone for a bit, and then begin on new lines. Poor children, it is no fault of theirs if they are not as they were meant to be—curious eager little souls, all agog to explore so much of this wonderful world as they can get at, as quite their first business in life.

> *"He prayeth best who loveth best*
> *All things both great and small;*
> *For the dear God who loveth us,*
> *He made and loveth all."*

Nature Knowledge the Most Important for Young Children

It would be well if we all persons in authority, parents and all who act for parents, could make up our minds that there is no sort of knowledge to be got in these early years so valuable to children as that which they get for themselves of the world they live in. Let them once get touch with Nature, and a habit is formed which will be a source of delight through life. We were all meant to be naturalists, each in his degree, and it is inexcusable to live in a world so full of the marvels of plant and animal life and to care for none of these things.

Mental Training of a Child Naturalist

Consider, too, what an unequalled mental training the child-naturalist is getting for any study or calling under the sun— the powers of attention, of discrimination, of patient pursuit, growing with his growth, what will they not fit him for? Besides, life is so interesting to him, that he has no time for the faults of temper which generally have their source in *ennui*; there is no reason why he should be peevish or sulky or obstinate when he is always kept well amused.

Nature Work Especially Valuable for Girls

I say 'he' from force of habit, as speaking of the representative sex, but truly that *she* should be thus conversant with Nature is a matter of infinitely more importance to the little girl: she it is who is most tempted to indulge in ugly tempers (as child and woman) because time hangs heavy on her hands; she, whose idler, more desultory habits of mind want the spur and bridle of an earnest absorbing pursuit; whose feebler health demands to be braced by an out-of-door life full of healthy excitement. Moreover, is it to the girls, little and big, a most true kindness to lift them out of themselves and out of the round of petty personal interests and emulations which too often hem in their lives; and then, with whom but the girls must it rest to mould the generations yet to be born?

7

FIELD-LORE AND NATURALISTS' BOOKS

Reverence for Life

Is it advisable, then, to teach the children the elements of natural science, of biology, botany, zoology? on the whole, no: the dissection even of a flower is painful to a sensitive child, and, during the first six or eight years of life, I would not teach them any botany which should necessitate the pulling of flowers to bits; much less should they be permitted to injure or destroy any (not noxious) form of animal life. Reverence for *life*, as a wonderful and awful gift, which a ruthless child may destroy but never can restore, is a lesson of first importance to the child:—

> *"Let knowledge grow from more to more;*
> *But more of reverence in us dwell."*

The child who sees his mother with reverent touch lift an early snowdrop to her lips, learns a higher lesson than the 'print-books' can teach. Years hence, when the children are old enough to understand that science itself is in a sense sacred and demands some sacrifices, all the 'common information' they have been gathering until then, and the habits of observation they have acquired, will form a capital groundwork for a scientific education.

In the meantime, let them *consider* the lilies of the field and the fowls of the air.

Rough Classification at First Hand

For convenience in describing they should be able to name and distinguish petals, sepals, and so on; and they should be encouraged to make such rough classifications as they can with their slight knowledge of both animal and vegetable forms. Plants with heart-shaped or spoon-shaped leaves, with whole or divided leaves; leaves with crisscross veins and leaves with straight veins; bell-shaped flowers and cross-shaped flowers; flowers with three petals, with four, with five; trees which keep their leaves all the year, and trees which lose them in autumn; creatures with a backbone and creatures without; creatures that eat grass and creatures that eat flesh, and so on. To make collections of leaves and flowers, pressed and mounted, and arranged according to their form, affords much pleasure, and, what is better, valuable training in the noticing of differences and resemblances. Patterns for this sort of classification of leaves and flowers will be found in every little book for elementary botany.

The power to classify, discriminate, distinguish between things that differ, is amongst the highest faculties of the human intellect, and no opportunity to cultivate it should be let slip; but a classification got out of books, that the child does not make for himself, cultivates no power but that of verbal memory, and a phrase or two of 'Tamil' or other unknown tongue, learnt off, would serve that purpose just as well.

Uses of 'Naturalists' ' Books

The real use of naturalists' books at this stage is to give the child delightful glimpses into the world of wonders he lives in, to reveal the sorts of things to be seen by curious eyes, and fill him with desire to make discoveries for himself. There are many[1] to be had, all pleasant reading, many of them written by scientific men, and yet requiring little or no scientific knowledge for the enjoyment.

Mothers and Teachers Should Know about Nature

The mother cannot devote herself too much to this kind of reading, not only that she may read tit-bits to her children about matters they have come across, but that she may be able to answer their queries and direct their observations. And not only the mother, but any woman, who is likely ever to spend an hour or two in the society of children, should make herself mistress of this sort of information; the children will adore her for knowing what they want to know, and who knows but she may give its bent for life to some young mind designed to do great things for the world.

8

WALKS IN BAD WEATHER

Winter Walks as Necessary as Summer Walks

All we have said hitherto applies to the summer weather, which is, alas for us! a very limited and uncertain quantity in our part of the world. The question of out-of-door exercise in winter and in wet weather is really more important; for who that could would not be abroad in the summer time? If the children are to have what is quite the best thing for them, they should be two or three hours every day in the open air all through winter, say an hour and a half in the morning and as long in the afternoon.

Pleasures Connected with Frost and Snow

When frost and snow are on the ground children have very festive times, what with sliding, snow-balling, and snow-building. But even on the frequent days when it is dirty under foot and dull overhead they should be kept interested and alert, so that the heart may do its work cheerfully, and a grateful glow be kept up throughout the body in spite of clouds and cold weather.

Winter Observations

All that has been said about 'sight-seeing' and 'picture painting,' the little French talk, and observations to be noted in the family diary, belongs just as much to winter weather as to summer; and there is no end to the things to be seen and noted. The party come across a big tree which they judge, from its build, to be an oak—down it goes in the diary; and when the leaves are out, the children come again to see if they are right. Many birds come into view the more freely in the cold weather that they are driven forth in search of food.

> *"The cattle mourn in corners where the fence screens them."*
> *"The sun, with ruddy orb*
> *Ascending, fires the horizon."*
> *"Every herb and every spiry blade*
> *Stretches a length of shadow o'er the field."*
> *"The sparrows peep, and quit the sheltering eaves.*
> *"The redbreast warbles still, but is content*
> *With slender notes, and more than half suppress'd;*
> *Pleased with his solitude, and flitting light*
> *From spray to spray, where'er he rests he shakes*
> *From many a twig the pendent drops of ice*
> *That tinkle in the wither'd leaves below."*

There is no reason why the child's winter walk should not be as fertile in observations as the poet's; indeed, in one way, it is possible to see the more in winter, because the things to be seen do not crowd each other out.

Habit of Attention

Winter walks, too, whether in town or country, give great opportunities for cultivating the habit of attention. The famous conjurer, Robert Houdin, relates in his autobiography, that he and his son would pass rapidly before a shop window, that of a toy shop, for instance, and each cast an attentive glance upon it. A few steps further on each drew paper and pencil from his pocket, and tried which could enumerate the greater number of the objects momentarily seen in passing. The boy surprised his father in quickness of apprehension, being often able to write down forty objects, whilst his father could scarcely reach thirty; yet on their returning to verify his statement, the son was rarely found to have made a mistake. Here is a hint for a highly educational amusement for many a winter's walk.

Wet Weather Tramps

But what about the wet days? The fact is, that rain, unless of the heaviest, does the children no harm at all if they are suitably clothed. But every sort of water proof garment should be tabooed, because the texture which will not admit rain will not allow of the escape of the insensible perspiration, and one secret of health for people who have no organic disease is the prompt carrying off of the decayed and harmful matters discharged by the skin.

Outer Garments

Children should have woolen rain-garments—made of coarse serge, for instance,—to be changed the moment they return from a walk, and then there is no risk of catching cold. This is the common-sense of the matter. Wet cloths are put upon the head of a fever patient; by-and-by the cloths dry, and are dipped again: what has become of the water? It has evaporated, and, in evaporating, has carried off much heat from the fevered head. Now, that which eases the hot skin of fever is just the one thing to be avoided in ordinary circumstances. To be wet to the skin may do a child no more harm than a bath would do him, if the wet clothes do not dry upon him—that is, if the water does not evaporate, carrying off much heat from his body in the process. It is the loss of animal heat which is followed by 'colds,' and not the 'wetting,' which mothers are ready to deplore. Keep an child active and happy in the rain, and he gets nothing but good from his walk. The case is altered if the child has a cold already; then active exercise might increase any inflammation already set up.

I do not know whether it is more than a pretty fancy of Richter's, that a spring shower is a sort of electric bath, and a very potent means of health; certainly rain clears the atmosphere—a fact of considerable importance in and about large towns. But it is enough for our purpose to prove that the rain need do no harm;

for abundant daily exercise in the fresh air is of such vital importance to the children, that really nothing but sickness should keep them within doors. A mere time and distance tramp is sufficiently joyous for a wet day, for, taken good-humouredly, the beating rain itself is exhilarating. The 'long run' of the schoolboy, that is, a steady trot, breaking now and then into a run, is capital exercise; but regard must be had to the powers of the children, who must not be overdone.

Precautions

At the same time, children should never be allowed to sit or stand about in damp clothes; and here is the use of waterproof rain-wraps—to keep them dry on short journeys to church, or school, or neighbour's house, where they cannot very well change their garments.

9

'RED INDIAN' LIFE

Scouting

Baden Powell's little book about *Scouting* set us upon a new track. Hundreds of families make joyous expeditions, far more educative than they dream, wherein scouting is the order of the day. For example, one party of four or more lies in ambush,—the best ambush to be had, which is pitched upon after much consideration. The enemy scouts; first he finds the ambush, and then his skill is shown in getting within touch of the alert foe without being discovered. But every family should possess *Scouting* in default of the chance of going on the war-path with a Red Indian. The evil of the ready-made life we lead is that we do not discern the signs of the times. An alert intelligence towards what goes on in the open-air world is a great possession, and, strongly as we sympathise with the effort made to put down bird's-nesting, we shall lose, if we are not careful, one of the few bits of what we may call 'Red Indian' training still within our reach.

Bird-stalking

But bird 'stalking,' to adapt a name, is a great deal more exciting and delightful than bird's nesting, and we get our joy at no cost of pain to other living things. All the skill of a good scout comes into play. Think, how exciting to creep noiselessy as shadows behind river-side bushes on hands and knees without disturbing a twig or pebble till you get within a yard of a pair of sandpipers, and then, lying low, to watch their dainty little runs, pretty tricks of head and tail, and to hear the music of their call.

And here comes the real joy of bird-stalking. If in the winter months the children have become fairly familiar with the notes of our resident birds, they will be able in the early summer to 'stalk' to some purpose. The notes and songs in June are quite bewildering, but the plan is to single out those you are quite sure of, and then follow up the others. The key to a knowledge of birds is knowledge of their notes, and the only way to get this is to follow any note of which you are not sure. The joy of tracking a song or note to its source is the joy of a 'find,' a possession for life.

But bird-stalking is only to be done upon certain conditions. You must not only be 'most mousy-quiet,' but you must not even let a thought whisper, for if you let yourself think about anything else, the entirely delightful play of bird-life passes by you unobserved; nay, the very bird notes are unheard.

Here are two bird walks communicated by a bird lover:—

"We heard a note something like a chaffinch's, only slower, and we looked up in the boughs of the ash to try and track the bird by the sudden quiver of one twig here, another, there. We found a steep, rocky path which brought us almost level with the tree tops, and then we had a good view of the shy little willow wren busily seeking food. A note from the next tree like a bubbling of song drew us farther on, and then we found the wood wren and watched him as with up-turned head and bubbling throat he uttered his trill."

"A joyous burst of song came from a bush nearby, and we crept on, to find a blackcap warbler with upraised crest turning excitedly round and round in the ecstasy of song. We waited, and traced him to his next station by his light touch on the branches. A hoarse screech from another tree announced a green-finch, and we had a long chase to get a glimpse of him; but he came to an outstanding twig, and then we heard his pretty song, which I should never have guessed to be his had we not seen him at it. A little squeaky note made us watch the tree trunks, and, sure enough, there was a tree-creeper running up and round and round an ash, uttering his note all the time.

"Another day we got behind a wall from which we could examine a field that lay beside the lake. There was the green plover with his jaunty crest, running and pecking, and, as he pecked, we caught sight of the rosy flash under his tail. We waited, hoping for more, for the plovers stand so still that they are lost in their surroundings. But someone coughed, and up went the plovers, a dozen of them, with their weary taunt, 'Why don't you let us alone?' Their distress roused other birds, and we saw a snipe rise from the water edge, a marshy place, with hasty zigzag flight; it made a long round and settled not much further than where it rose. The sandpipers rose, two flying close to the water's edge, whistling all the time. By the side of a little gully we watched a wagtail, and presently a turn in the sunshine showed us the yellow breast of the yellow wagtail. A loud 'tis-sic' near us drew our eyes to the wall, and there stood a pied wagtail with full beak, waiting to get rid of us before visiting his nest in the wall. We crept away and sheltered behind a tree, and after a few minutes' waiting we saw him go into his hole. An angry chatter nearby (like a broom on Venetian blinds!) directed our eyes to a little brown wren on the wall with cocked-up tail, but in a minute he disappeared like a mouse over the side."

This from another bird-lover:—

"Now, they (the children) are beginning to care more for the birds than the eggs, and their first question, instead of being, 'What is the egg like?' is usually 'What is the bird like?' We have great searching through Morris's *British Birds*[3] to identify birds we have seen and to make quite sure of doubtful points. "But now for the birds. *Stonechats* abound on the heaths. I pricked myself up to my knees standing in a gorse-patch watching and listening to the first I saw, but I was quite rewarded, and saw at least four pairs at one time. Do you know the birds? The cock-birds are such handsome little fellows, black head and mask, white collar, rufous breast and dark grey or brown back. They have a pretty little song, rather longer than a chaffinch's, besides the chit-chat cry when they are disturbed. They do not make a long flight, and will hover in the air like a flycatcher. The sandmartins have numbers of holes in the cliffs. We tried to see how deep they burrowed to build their nests, but though I put my arm in up to the elbows in several deserted holes, I could not reach the end. I think my favourites are the reed-warblers. I know of at least four pairs, and when I could induce the children to *both* stop talking for a few minutes, we were able to watch them boldly hopping up and down the reeds and singing in full view of us."

This is the sort of thing bird-stalkers come upon—and what a loss have those children who are not brought up to the gentle art wherein the eye is satisfied with seeing, and there is no greed of collecting, no play of the hunter's instinct to kill, and yet a lifelong joy of possession.

10

THE CHILDREN REQUIRE COUNTRY AIR

The Essential Proportion of Oxygen

Everyone knows that the breathing of air which has lost little of its due proportion of oxygen is the essential condition of vigorous life and of a fine physique; also, that whatever produces heat, whether it be animal heat, or the heat of fire, candle, gas-lamp, produces that heat at the expense of the oxygen in the atmosphere—a bank which is drawn upon by every breathing and burning object; that in situations where much breathing and burning are going on, there is a terrible drain upon this vital gas; that the drain may be so excessive that there no longer sufficient oxygen in the air to support animal life, and death results; that where the drain is less excessive but still great, animal life may be supported, and people live in a flaccid, feeble life in a state of low vitality.

Excess of Carbonic Acid Gas

Also we know that every breathing and every burning object expels a hurtful gas—carbonic acid. A very small proportion of this gas is present in the purest atmospheric air, and that small proportion is healthful; but increase that quantity by the action of furnaces, fires, living beings, gas-lamps, and the air is rendered unwholesome, just in proportion to the quantity of superfluous carbonic-acid gas it contains. If the quantity be excessive—as when many people are huddled together in a small unventilated room— speedy death by suffocation is the result.

Unvitiated, Unimpoverished Air

For these reasons, it is not possible to enjoy fullness of life in a town. For grown-up people, the stimulus of town life does something to make up for the impurity of town air; as, on the other hand, country people too often forfeit their advantages through the habit of mental sluggishness they let themselves fall into: but, for the children—who not only breathe, but grow; who require, proportionately, more oxygen than adults need for their vital processes—it is absolutely cruel not to give them very frequent, if not daily, copious draughts of unvitiated, unimpoverished air, the sort of air that can be had only remote from towns.

Solar Light

But this is only one of the reasons why, for health's sake alone, it is of the first importance to give children long days in the open country. They want light, solar light, as well as air. Country people are ruddier than town folk; miners are sallow, so are the dwellers in cellars and in sunless valleys. The reason is, that, to secure the ruddy glow of perfect health, certain changes must take place in the blood—the nature of which it would take too long to explain here—and that these changes in the blood, marked by free production of red corpuscles, appear to take place most favourably under the influence of abundant solar light. What is more, men of science are beginning to suspect that not only the coloured light rays of the solar spectrum, but the dark heat rays, and the chemical rays, minister to vitality in ways not yet fully understood.

A Physical Ideal for a Child

There was a charming picture in *Punch* some time ago, of two little boys airing their English-French on their mother's new maid; two noble little fellows, each straight as a dart, with no superfluous flesh, eyes well opened, head erect, chest expanded, the whole body full of spring even in repose. It was worth looking at, if only as suggesting the sort of physique we delight to see in a child. No doubt the child inherits the most that he is in this respect as in all others; but *this* is what bringing-up may, with some limitations, effect:—The child is born with certain natural tendencies, and, according to his bringing-up, each such tendency may run into a blemish of person or character, or into a cognate grace. Therefore, it is worthwhile to have even a *physical* ideal for one's child; not, for instance, to be run away with by the notion that a fat child is necessarily a fine child. The fat child can easily be produced: but the bright eyes, the open regard, the springing step; the tones, clear as a bell; the agile, graceful movements that characterize the well-brought-up child, are the result, not of bodily well-being only, but of 'mind and soul according well,' of a quick, trained intelligence, and of a moral nature habituated to the 'joy of self-control.'

11

TEACHING NATURAL PHILOSOPHY

A Basis of Facts

Of the teaching of *Natural Philosophy*, I will only remind the reader of what was said in an earlier chapter—that there is no part of a child's education more important than that he should lay, by his own observation, a wide basis of *facts* towards scientific knowledge in the future. He must live hours daily in the open air, and, as far as possible, in the country; must look and touch and listen; must be quick to note, *consciously*, every peculiarity of habit or structure, in beast, bird, or insect; the manner of growth and fructification of every plant.

He must be accustomed to ask *why*—Why does the wind blow? Why does the river flow? Why is a leaf-bud sticky? And do not hurry to answer his questions for him; let him think his difficulties out so far as his small experience will carry him. Above all, when you come to the rescue, let it not be in the 'cut and dried' formula of some miserable little text-book; let him have all the insight available and you will find that on many scientific questions the child may be brought at once to the level of modern thought.

Do not embarrass him with too much scientific nomenclature. If he discover for himself (helped, perhaps, by a leading question or two), by comparing an oyster and his cat, that some animals have backbones and some have not, it is less important that he should learn the terms vertebrate and invertebrate than that he should class the animals he meets with according to this difference.

Eyes and No-eyes

The *method* of this sort of instruction is shown in *Evenings at Home*, where 'Eyes and No-eyes' go for a walk. No-eyes come home bored; he has seen nothing, been interested in nothing: while Eyes is all agog to discuss a hundred things that have interested him. As I have already tried to point out, to get this sort of instruction for himself is simply the *nature* of a child: the business of the parent is to afford him abundant and varied opportunities, and to direct his observations, so that, knowing little of the principles of scientific classification, he is, unconsciously, furnishing himself with the materials for such classification. It is needless to repeat what has already been said on this subject; but, indeed, the future of the man or woman depends very largely on the store of real knowledge gathered, and the habits of intelligent observation acquired, by the child. "Think you," says Mr. Herbert Spencer, "that the rounded rock marked with parallel scratches calls up as much poetry in an ignorant mind as in the mind of the geologist, who knows that over this rock a glacier slid a million of years ago? The truth is, that those who have never entered on scientific pursuits are blind to most of the poetry by which they are surrounded. Whoever has not in youth collected plants and insects, knows not half the halo of interest which lanes and hedgerows can assume."

Principles

In this connection I should like to recommend *The Sciences*, by Mr. Holden. America comes to the fore with a schoolbook after my own heart. *The Sciences* is a forbidding title, but since the era of Joyce's *Scientific Dialogues* I have met with nothing on the same lines which makes so fit an approach to the sensible and intelligent mind of a child. This is what we may call a 'first-hand' book. The knowledge has of course all been acquired; but then it has been assimilated, and Mr. Holden writes freely out of his own knowledge both of his subject-matter and of his readers. The book has been thrown into the form of conversations between children—simple conversations without padding. About three hundred topics are treated of: Sand-dunes, Back-ice, Herculaneum, Dredging, Hurricanes, Echoes, the Prism, the Diving-bell, the Milky Way, and, shall I say, everything else? But the amazing skill of the author is shown in the fact that there is nothing scrappy and nothing hurried in the treatment of any topic, but each falls naturally and easily under the head of some principle which it elucidates. Many simple experiments are included, which the author insists shall be performed by the children themselves. I venture to quote from the singularly wise preface, a *vade mecum* for teachers:—

"The object of the present volume is to present chapters to be read in school or at home that shall materially widen the outlook of American schoolchildren in the domain of science, and of the applications of science to the arts and to daily life. It is in no sense a text-book, although the fundamental principles underlying the sciences treated are here laid down. Its main object is to help the child to understand the material world about him.

To be Comprehended by Children

"All natural phenomena are orderly; they are governed by law; they are not magical. They are comprehended by someone; why not by the child himself? It is not possible to explain every detail of a locomotive to a young pupil, but it is perfectly practicable to explain its principles so that this machine, like others, becomes a mere special case of certain well-understood general laws. The general plan of the book is to awaken the imagination; to convey useful knowledge; to open the doors towards wisdom. Its special aim is to stimulate observation and to excite a living and lasting interest in the world that lies about us.

"The sciences of astronomy, physics, chemistry, meteorology, and physiography are treated as fully and as deeply as the conditions permit; and the lessons that they teach are enforced by examples taken from familiar and important things. In astronomy, for example, emphasis is laid upon phenomena that the child himself can observe, and he is instructed how to go about it. The rising and setting of the stars, the phases of the moon, the uses of the telescope, are explained in simple words. The mystery of these and other matters is not magical, as the child at first supposes. It is to deeper mysteries that his attention is here directed. Mere phenomena are treated as special cases of very general laws. The same process is followed in the exposition of the other sciences.

"Familiar phenomena, like those of steam, of shadows, of reflected light, of musical instruments, of echoes, etc., are referred to their fundamental causes. Whenever it is desirable, simple experiments are described and fully illustrated, and all such experiments can very well be repeated in the schoolroom. . . . The volume is the result of a sincere belief that much can be done to aid young children to comprehend the material world in which they live, and of a desire to have a part in a work so very well worth doing."

I cannot help quoting also in this connection from an article[1] by the Rev. H. H. Moore dealing with a forgotten pioneer of a rational education and his experiment. This pioneer was the Rev. Richard Dawes, at one time Rector of Kings Somborne parish, Hampshire, who, in 1841, worked out the problem of rational education in an agricultural village, in which he found the population unusually ignorant and debased. The whole story is of great interest, but our concern is with the question of Natural Philosophy, the staple of the teaching given in this school.

As Taught in a Village School

Mr. Dawes thus Explained his Object:

"I aimed at teaching what would be profitable and interesting to persons in the position in life which the children were likely to occupy. I aimed at their being taught what may be called the philosophy of common things of everyday life. They were shown how much there is that is interesting, and which it is advantageous for them to know, in connection with the natural objects with which they are familiar; they had explained to them, and were made acquainted with, the principles of a variety of natural phenomena, as well as the principles and construction of various instruments of a useful kind. A practical turn was given to everything the uses and fruits of the knowledge they were acquiring were never lost sight of." A list of some of the subjects included in this kind of teaching will be the best commentary on Mr. Dawes' scheme:—

"Some of the properties of air, explaining how its pressure enables them to pump up water, to amuse themselves with squirts and popguns, to suck up water through a straw; explaining also the principles and construction of a barometer, the common pump, the diving-bell, a pair of bellows. That air expands by heat, shown by placing a half-blown bladder near the fire, when the wrinkles disappear. Why the chimney-smoke sometimes rises easily in the air, sometimes not; why there is a draught up the chimney, and under the door, and towards the fire. Air as a vehicle of sound, and why the flash of a distant gun fired is seen before the report is heard; how to calculate the distance of a thunderstorm; the difference in the speeds at which different materials conduct sound.

"Water and its properties, its solid, fluid, and vaporous state; why water-pipes are burst by frost; why ice forms and floats on the surface of ponds, and not at the bottom; why the kettle-lid jumps up when the water is boiling on the fire; the uses to which the power of steam is applied; the gradual evolution of the steam-engine, shown by models and diagrams; how their clothes are dried, and why they feel cold sitting in damp clothes; why a damp bed is so dangerous; why one body floats in water, and another sinks; the different densities of sea and fresh water; why, on-going into the school on a cold morning, they sometimes see a quantity of water on the glass, and why on the inside and not on the outside; why, on a frosty day, their breath is visible as vapour; the substances water holds in solution, and how their drinking water is affected by the kind of soil through which it has passed. Dew, its value, and the conditions necessary for its formation; placing equal portions of dry wool on gravel, glass, and the grass, and weighing them the next morning.

"Heat and its properties; how it is that the blacksmith can fit iron hoops so firmly on the wheels of carts and barrows; what precautions have to be taken in laying the iron rails of railways and in building iron bridges, etc.; what materials are good, and what bad, conductors of heat; why at the same temperature some feel colder to our touch than others; why a glass sometimes breaks when hot water is poured into it, and whether thick or thin glass would be more liable to crack; why water can be made to boil in a paper kettle or an eggshell without its being burned.

"The metals, their sources, properties, and uses; mode of separating from the ores. Light and its properties, illustrated by prisms, etc; adaptation of the eye; causes of long and short-sightedness. The mechanical principles of the tools more commonly used, the spade, the plough, the axe, the lever, etc."

It may surprise some who read carefully the above list that such subjects should have been taught to the children of a rural elementary school. But it is an undeniable fact that they were taught in Kings Somborne School, and so successfully that the children were both interested and benefited by the teaching. Mr. Dawes, in answer to the objection that such subjects are above the comprehension of the young, said:—

'The distinguishing mark of Nature's laws is their extreme simplicity. It may doubtless require intellect of a high order to make the discovery of these laws; yet, once evolved, they are within the capacity of a child,—in short, the principles of natural philosophy are the principles of common sense, and if taught in a simple and common-sense way, they will be speedily understood and eagerly attended to by children; and it will be found that with pupils of even from ten to twelve years of age much may be done towards forming habits of observation and inquiry.' Such a fact, I think, suggests some valuable practical lessons for those who have the responsibility of deciding what subjects to include in an educational system for children."

In reading of this remarkable experiment, we feel that we must at once secure a man, all-informed like the late Dean Dawes, to teach our own Jack and Elsie; but it is something to realise what these young persons should know, and Mr. Holden has done a great deal for us. Some of the chapters in *The Sciences* may be beyond children under nine, but they will be able to master a good deal. One thing is to be borne in mind: nothing should be done without its due experiment. By the way, our old friend, Joyce's *Scientific Dialogues*, if it is still to be had, describes a vast number of easy and interesting experiments which children can work for themselves.

Science

In *Science*, or rather, nature study, we attach great importance to *recognition*, believing that the power to recognise and name a plant or stone or constellation involves classification and includes a good deal of knowledge. To know a plant by its gesture and habitat, its time and its way of flowering and fruiting; a bird by its flight and song and its times of coming and going; to know when, year after year, you may come upon the redstart and the pied fly-catcher, means a good deal of interested observation, and of, at any rate, the material for science.

The children keep a dated record of what they see in their nature note-books, which are left to their own management and are not corrected. These note-books are a source of pride and joy, and are freely illustrated by drawings (brushwork) of twig, flower, insect, etc. The knowledge necessary for these records is not given in the way of teaching. On one afternoon in the week, the children (of the Practising School) go for a 'nature walk' with their teachers. They notice for themselves, and the teacher gives a name or other information as it is asked for, and it is surprising what a range of knowledge a child of nine or ten acquires.

The teachers are careful *not* to make these nature walks an opportunity for scientific instruction, as we wish the children's attention to be given to observation with very little direction. In this way they lay up that store of 'common information' which Huxley considered should precede science teaching; and, what is much more important, they learn to know and delight in natural objects as in the familiar faces of friends. The nature-walk should not be made the occasion to impart a sort of *Tit-Bits* miscellany of scientific information. The study of science should be pursued in an ordered sequence, which is not possible or desirable in a walk. It seems to me a *sine quâ non* of a living education that all school children of whatever grade should have one half-day in the week, *throughout the year*, in the fields. There are few towns where country of some sort is not accessible, and every child should have the opportunity of watching from week to week, the procession of the seasons.

Geography, geology, the course of the sun, the behaviour of the clouds, weather signs, all that the 'open' has to offer, are made use of in these walks; but all is incidental, easy, and things are noticed as they occur. It is probable that in most neighbourhoods there are naturalists who would be willing to give their help in the 'nature walks' of a given school.

We supplement this direct 'nature walk' by occasional object-lessons, as, on the hairs of plants, on diversity of wings, on the sorts of matters taken up in Professor Miall's capital books; but our main dependence is on *books* as an adjunct to out-of-door work—Mrs. Fisher's, Mrs. Brightwen's, Professor Lloyd Morgan's, Professor Geikie's, Professors Geddes' and Thomson's (the two last for children over fourteen), etc., etc. In the books of these and some other authors the children are put in the position of the original observer of biological and other phenomena. They learn what to observe, and make discoveries for themselves, original so far as they are concerned. They are put in the right attitude of mind for scientific observations and deductions, and their keen interest is awakened.

We are extremely careful not to burden the verbal memory with scientific nomenclature. Children learn of pollen, antennae, and what not, incidentally, when the thing is present and they require a name for it. The children who are curious about it, and they only, should have the opportunity of seeing with the microscope any minute wonder of structure that has come up in their reading or their walks; but a good lens is a capital and almost an indispensable companion in field work. I think there is danger in giving *too* prominent a place to education by Things, enormous as is its value; a certain want of atmosphere is apt to result, and a deplorable absence of a standard of comparison and of the principle of veneration. 'We are the people!' seems to be the note of an education which is not largely sustained on *books* as well as on *things*.

ABOUT THE EDITOR

Deborah Taylor-Hough, long-time homeschooling mother of three (now adult) children, is the author of a number of popular books including *Frugal Living For Dummies*® and the bestselling *Frozen Assets* cookbook series. Debi also worked as Outreach Director and Youth Director at her church, and regularly teaches classes, workshops and seminars throughout the USA and Canada to women's groups, conferences, churches, and community education programs.

Debi's workshop topics include:

- Charlotte Mason home education
- living within your means
- simple living
- cooking for the freezer
- general homemaking
- writing, publishing and publicity
- identifying personal priorities
- simplifying the holidays
- easy educational ideas for children
- ... and more!

Visit Debi online:

CharlotteMasonHome.com
TheSimpleMom.com

Also available from Deborah Taylor-Hough:

Frozen Assets: Cook for a Day, Eat for a Month
ISBN: 9781402218590 (Sourcebooks)
This breakthrough cookbook delivers a program for readers to cook a week or a month's worth of meals in just one day by using easy and affordable recipes to create a customized meal plan. The author, who saved $24,000 on her family's total grocery bill during a five-year period, offers up kid-tested and family approved recipes in Frozen Assets, plus bulk-cooking tips for singles, shopping lists, recipes for two-week and 30-day meal plans, and a ten-day plan to eliminate cooking over the holidays. Cooking for the freezer allows you to plan ahead, purchase items in bulk, cut down on waste, and stop those all-too-frequent trips to the drive-thru.

Frozen Assets Lite and Easy
ISBN: 9781402218606 (Sourcebooks)
Taylor-Hough is back with a book of low-fat, lower-calorie meal plans that use the same time-saving and cost-effective methods. *Frozen Assets Lite and Easy* shows readers how to eat healthy food while still saving time and money, with shopping lists, recipes, and detailed instruction on how to make freezer cooking work for you.

Frugal Living For Dummies®
ISBN: 9780764554032 (Wiley)
Need help keeping that New Year's resolution to eliminate credit card debt and live within your means? Packed with tips on cutting costs on everything from groceries to gifts for all occasions, this practical guide shows you how to spend less on the things you need and save more for those fun things you want.

Made in the USA
Las Vegas, NV
28 February 2021

18765814R00039